M.G. Van Rensselaer

In the heart of the Alleghenies

historical and descriptive

M.G. Van Rensselaer

In the heart of the Alleghenies
historical and descriptive

ISBN/EAN: 9783744735667

Printed in Europe, USA, Canada, Australia, Japan

Cover: Foto ©ninafisch / pixelio.de

More available books at **www.hansebooks.com**

IN THE HEART OF THE ALLEGHENIES.

HISTORICAL AND DESCRIPTIVE.

BY

M. G. VAN RENSSELAER.

PHILADELPHIA.

1885.

In the Heart of the Alleghenies.

ON THE WAY.

THE White Mountains and the Green Mountains, the Adirondacks and the Catskills, are all well known to the tourists from our Eastern cities. Even the most confirmed stay-at-home cannot be unacquainted with their charms,—with the nature of their beauty and the interest of their traditions,—so fully have they been written about during a long course of years. But the Alleghenies, though as accessible as any of our mountain-ranges, and as beautiful in their way, are far less familiar to the health-seeker, the lover of the picturesque, and the reader of popular literature. They are looked upon, I fear, by the majority of those who approach their base, merely in the light of obstructions in a transcontinental journey. A few moments spent in wondering admiration of the "Horseshoe Curve" is perhaps the only tribute to their beauty paid by the average traveler. Broad reaches of rolling hill-tops lie outspread before him, deep, narrow gaps and gorges run at right angles to the railroad, offering vistas of the most seductive loveliness; but the country is not a fashionable resort for tourists, and the fame of its beauties is but local. So the traveler goes on his way indifferent, until chance or necessity, perhaps, forces upon him the introduction he would not seek. Dull and blind he must be, however, if more than a first experience is necessary to make him a lover of these mountains and a singer of their beauty ever after. Their physical charms, moreover, are supplemented by an historical record, which, in spite of the fact that it falls almost entirely within the present century, is not deficient in the romantic and adventurous incidents which mark the earlier history of places farther East.

In order to get a sort of bird's-eye view of the district that shall fix its main features in our mind for reference when we come to speak in detail of things that are and things that were, let us first take a day-train from Harrisburg and go with it up to the mountain-top, past Cresson, and down again on the other side. The road we follow is the chief artery of the State of Pennsylvania, the channel through which flows the main current of its vast activity. But it is much more than a great local highway. It is also one of the chief lines by which the East and the West join hands across the continent. The history of this railroad in its first beginnings, as we shall trace them later on, is a curious record not only of local enterprise but of early experiments in "railroading" as well. It is but fifty years since those experiments were begun, yet the first road over the Alleghenies has been superseded and done away with. It has, indeed, passed not only out of use but almost out of mind. How many of the thousand daily passengers over the present track know that there was another steam-route—yes, two others—that preceded it? Even the picturesque remains of the pioneer road—does it seem strange to talk of "remains" in connection with anything so new as railroads, and of picturesqueness as a visible element therein?—are as nearly forgotten as their history, both alike being known to few but local antiquaries and the summer-boarders of the neighborhood, who are very generally from localities not far away.

Leaving Harrisburg, with its outlying iron-works, which prophesy of the vast coal and iron industries that will meet us at every turn, our road follows the Susquehanna to its junction with the Juniata, and then clings for many miles to the beautiful banks of the latter stream. Noteworthy, even in comparison with the grandeur to come, when we shall reach the highest range,—the Allegheny proper,—are these smaller ranges. Most exquisite, especially, is the gap where the Juniata breaks through its detaining hills. When Blair County is almost reached, the road curves to the north and then trends sharply in a southerly direction, so that we run into Altoona between two of the long north-and-south mountain ridges. Altoona is the metropolis of the mountains and the chief home of their iron industry in its second stage. Here the half-earthen mass is not taken in all its disheartening crudeness to be forced by the main strength of gigantic fires into shapely cubes of tractable material, but this already docile material is laid hold of for further educating, and is half coerced, half persuaded, seemingly, by machines that are almost human, nay, superhuman, in their working, into shapes whose variety, delicacy, strength, and accuracy are something more than marvelous. In a word, this is not the city of iron-works proper, but of "shops," in the technical sense,—places which the visitor will find very unlike the haunts of femininity usually suggested by the word. These at Altoona are the railroad-shops,—labyrinthine, deafening, oleaginous, magical, fascinating birth-places of engine and of car.

Passing on our road towards the places and things which just now more especially interest us, we begin the ascent of the Allegheny itself. Traversing the thirty-eight miles which lie between Altoona at the foot of the final ridge toward the east, and Johnstown, which we shall find at its western base, we are bewildered by a succession of magnificent views and splendid triumphs of engineering skill. Nature and man alike have done their best at the famous Horseshoe Curve. Famous it is most justly. I have seen many magnificent roads in the older world, passes of Alps and Apennines, where the background of surrounding peaks is far sublimer and the panorama extends itself over many more miles of length,—places, too, where the engineer had even harder problems to solve than here. But all the same I can recollect no one spot where the road takes so superb a line and where the work of man so seems to but complete an original intention of nature herself. We have been told often enough that railroads are the devil's work when they meddle with nature that is sublime or lovely. But here, at least, the iron line and steed seem as if invented by some æsthetically-minded Titan to fit a route no other steed could so appropriately travel.

The wonderful curve being passed, the road still carries us up and up, along a line scarcely less bold and beautiful, till we suddenly plunge into a long tunnel, which, piercing as it does the loftiest peak we shall touch, brings us to our highest level. We run out into the light again at Gallitzin,—a curious name, we think, to meet us here amid relics of Indian nomenclature and titles derived from the modern industries of fire and iron. In it, with its strange suggestion of things foreign, warlike, and here most alien, we have our first introduction to the man who was settler and evangelizer of the country hereabouts. Insignificant though it be in itself, Gallitzin is yet the topmost point of the great highway, and so does him good and merited service in forcing his name upon the notice, and his memory upon the mind of every traveler from east to west and from west to east. From Gallitzin we run along a mile or so to Cresson, and thence, by descending grades less steep and less boldly picturesque than those of the eastern slope, glide down to Johnstown, where our westward journey is to end.

CRESSON SPRINGS.

Cresson Spings is not a village even. It is but the "Mountain House," with its cluster of dependent cottages, space for which has been cleared in a natural grove, principally of maple trees. There are said to be three miles of well-laid-out walks and drives within the hotel-grounds, while beyond those grounds, on more sides than one, we have the almost untouched forest before us. The winding little paths that have been cut for our benefit here and there scarcely affect the primitive wildness of its aspect. The place is owned by the railroad, and one of its chief recommendations is the fact that it is in such easy communication with the rest of the world. The mails come and go at all hours, and every passenger-train bound east or west stops before its door. The grounds of the hotel reach down to the track, but the hotel itself is at the top of a gentle slope, and so shut off by trees that there is no unpleasantness in the proximity. The weather is usually of delicious coolness,—for are we not two thousand feet above the sea? The country is exquisite for walking or driving, but especially for riding purposes. The abundant springs which supply the house are as pure as water can be, and their negative virtues are supplemented by the curative power of the iron springs which have long been known to the faculty. Although a room in the hotel proper would scarcely be the place for study, I can imagine no better headquarters for a student who desired either to work or to rest than one of the pretty cottages with shady porches that are close at hand. I can speak from experience of many long weeks spent in such a one. Books were plenty; hammocks swung under the trees conduced to study or to laziness with happy impartiality; there was all the privacy of a summer home with absolutely no care for the morrow. Only, the hospitable private cottages, with their custom of mid-day tea, and all-day cordiality, were rather subversive of good resolves as to spending one's morning in a profitably busy retirement.

The great drawback to the picturesqueness of the neighborhood is the entire lack of visible water, incident to a position at the very crest of a water-shed, and this lack deprives one, of course, of that chief delight in some mountain-districts,—facilities for boating and fishing. It must be confessed, indeed, that there is very little "to do" at Cresson in the way the term is understood by the energetic pleasure-seeker. The big new hotel built in 1881 has provided, it is true, greater social resources of a general character than were to be found in the quaint old building which till then had borne the name of Mountain House. For the railroad and for the average guest the change is undoubtedly for the better, as it is for every one in the way of physical comfort. But to some of us the "improvements" have lessened the attraction that Cresson offered in its humbler days. It is now a place like many others. It was then unique in its way to those who had been long accustomed to the caravansaries of our Eastern coast, though very likely not to such as were more familiar with the nooks and corners of the Pennsylvania hills. It is no longer what it was once called, the "Pittsburgh Nursery," peopled almost exclusively by a sociable coterie from the Smoky City in search of health and pleasure for troops of pretty children. It is no longer a place where an unaccustomed face was a rarity, and won, therefore, a more friendly greeting than can now be given when the great house is crowded with visitors from every part of the West and South. The private cottages still house the same kind Pittsburghers, but their individuality and coherence are swamped in the foreign throng.

When seeking information as to the origin and history of Cresson, I was referred to a gentleman who was said to be "a perfect magazine of Pennsylvanian history." By this happy chance I was introduced to the memory of a man who deserved at least a passing word of tribute from every lover of the Allegheny.

"Cresson itself," runs a part of my correspondent's answer, "was the outcome of the Pennsylvania Railroad, and was born of the brain and energy of my friend Dr. R. M. S. Jackson, a man of genius and fine culture, who once made his home on that wild mountain. He was a physician, a geologist, a mineralogist, and, indeed, a scientist of wide and accurate knowledge. An enthusiastic love of mountain-life led him to make his home on the old highway near Cresson when the railroad was being built, and, conceiving the idea of establishing a great sanitary institution on the mountain, he, with Mr. J. Edgar Thomson, purchased the tract of land now Cresson Springs and induced the directors of the railroad to transport to its present location at Cresson the building which had been their hotel at the foot of the mountain. He was a friend of Leidy, Leslie, and many other eminent naturalists. His house on the mountain, since destroyed by fire, was the resort of many of the most distinguished literary and scientific men of the day, and among his correspondents were Emerson, Dr. Furness, and Charles Sumner, whom he entertained for a month, in September, 1856, when he was suffering from the blows inflicted by Brooks, of South Carolina, in the Senate-chamber. In fact, his treatment, as Sumner often told me afterward, first put him on the way of such restored health as he ever had.

"Jackson wrote a most curious and interesting book called 'The Mountain,' full of practical and scientific information about that region, its flora, fauna, its springs, climatology, etc., and to prove that it was the great sanitarium of America. His dream was to make Cresson the resort and the place of restoration for all forms of human suffering; but protracted litigation with unsympathizing natives who challenged his title, and the usual unbusiness-like habits of a man of genius, plunged him into financial difficulties which defeated his purpose by depriving him of his interest in the property.

But, for all that, Cresson, with whatever of attraction it has, is the offspring of Jackson's conception and efforts. He had hoped to be surgeon-in-charge there, but, with characteristic enthusiasm, when the war broke out, in 1861, he offered his services as surgeon of a marching and fighting regiment of Pennsylvania volunteers, and, after an active and toilsome experience on many a well-fought field, he died, being then surgeon-in-charge of the extensive hospital on Lookout Mountain. How much you Cresson people have lost by his death !"

From the Mountain House itself there is no very extended view to be had, embowered in trees as it is, and occupying a shallow valley just below the highest hill-top. If we take the Hollidaysburg turnpike, however, which crosses the railroad just by the hotel and climbs the hill behind it, we shall find, when half a mile or so has brought us to the hill-top, that we have reached the little village of Summitville. From the level crest just back of "The Summit," as the place is called in local parlance, we have a wonderful view, by which we can judge as to what is the peculiar type of Allegheny beauty. For mountain-ranges are as individual as is the outline of any solitary peak, and there is one glory of the Adirondacks and another glory of the Alleghenies. There is far less grandeur of a wild sort here,—no commanding peaks, and little boldness of outline. But what is lost in wildness is gained in harmony and grace. The views in this region are very varied, of course. There are points not far away whence we get a sight of some of the numerous "gaps,"—of valleys deep and narrow, or very broad and sloping. But such a prospect as this one from the summit is peculiarly characteristic of the Allegheny. Looking northward over the shallow depression where Cresson lies and the railroad runs, we see nothing but a reach of high-rolling table-land. But what a reach it is!—so vast and broad and gently broken by the multitudinous round hill-tops that it seems as if our power of vision had been enlarged so as to embrace a myriad miles. There never was such a chance for color to show itself in all the tender grades of brown and green and yellow, unified by the blue haze of distance and the gray and purple shadows of the clouds. It is these last which give the crowning charm to the landscape. They have full sweep over the wonderful wide highlands, and by their magic the conformation of its surface seems to alter in the most marvelous and inexplicable way moment by moment as we watch.

The drives are very beautiful through all this region. It is hard to say which are the more lovely, the open highways, where the eye sweeps the far-receding hill-tops, or the narrow, dark, and odorous tunnels through the forest primeval. Its forests are the best glory of the Allegheny. In some parts where they are comparatively open, as on the drive to Gallitzin, parallel with the railroad, but a mile or so farther south, the undergrowth of ferns is splendid in its profusion.

THE PORTAGE ROAD—Old and New.

If we try now the turnpike from the Summit to Hollidaysburg, we shall find a road so steep and so rough with stones that our progress will be but slow. But the scenery is beautiful and in the greatest contrast to the broad panorama that was spread before us at the Summit. We are climbing down the cleft called Blair's Gap, the highest pass, I believe, through the Allegheny, and the mountain-tops rise steep and close on either side of us. Before we have gone very far, certain things will meet our eye that are not a usual sight in a district so new as this. We are not apt to find ruins of any kind in this fatherland of ours, and it seems doubly extraordinary to find them here in the wilderness, and to find them so picturesque. What was the origin, one cannot but wonder, of the isolated stone viaduct-arches that we pass, now going over one and now under the other? What is the meaning of yonder vast piece of masonry which shores up, as it were, the mountain-side, and seems to have supported a road which climbed around and clung to that narrow ledge so far above our heads! Why were such things built in this thinly-peopled place? and, if they were needed, why have they so soon served all their purpose and been given over into the hands of time and of neglect? Our driver, whether indigenous or merely attached to Cresson by a long course of summer-visiting, is sure to take an interest in the local antiquities, and there will be a touch of pride in his voice as he tells us that all these things were once part and parcel of the "Old Portage Road." There may also be a hint of scorn or incredulity in his look when he finds that his information does not enlighten us very much, but that we are still rather vague and unimpressed.

Let us now take another road from the Summit and drive westward for four or five miles toward the mining village of Lilly. Was there ever such a misnomer, by the way, for a gritty, grimy, hideous little town, where it is hard to say which are the blacker, the people or their habitations? We have followed hither a broad highway, which, to keep an approximate level, cuts more than once through the elevations along its way. The road is broader and more carefully graded than is usual with the turnpikes hereabouts, and in many places, moreover, we see large square blocks of stone embedded in the highway a few feet from each other. This road too, we shall be told, with other similar stretches between this and Johnstown, was once a part of the "Old Portage."

If we try at last to understand just what was this highway,—which in the year 1835 is said to have carried twenty thousand passengers and fifty thousand tons of freight, that being the first season of its completed existence, and travel only possible while the canals that joined it were open,—we shall find some difficulty in getting accurate information. It was a system of planes and levels, we shall be told, where cars were drawn up and let down the inclines by means of ropes, and even canal-boats transferred over the top of the Allegheny,—so that a craft which had been launched in the Chesapeake might ultimately find itself in the Gulf of Mexico. This brings us, by the way, to note the fact that at Cresson and the Summit we are at the very ridge of the water-shed which divides the great drainage-system of the eastern coast from that of the Mississippi Valley. The hollows and dells of the neighborhood discharge their waters in opposite directions with apparent causelessness ; and there is a place on the little branch-road from Cresson to Ebensburg where two springs are pointed out on opposite sides of the track, one of which contributes its mite to the Eastern and the other to the Southern system.

But to return to the Portage. Local information is so vague, proud as the natives are of their ruins,—for things are soon forgotten in this progressive land, where fifty years makes them thrice antiquated,—that we shall have to look for some printed source whence to get our facts. Even this is not readily to be found. That there should be no popular and easily-accessible account of such a work as this proves how completely it has been neglected by lovers of the picturesque as well as by those curious in the history of early engineering and of the enterprise and pluck of a generation past. It is to be hoped that my readers will pardon a page or two of what some may call rather "dry" reading ; for the undertaking of which we are to speak seems to me of sufficient interest and importance to warrant a little serious description.

In the year 1830 a canal was completed from Pittsburgh to Johnstown, at the western base of the main ridge of the Alleghenies. Eighty-two miles of railroad ran from Philadelphia to Columbia, and thence another canal went as far as Hollidaysburg, which was at the eastern slope of the range in question. Now, if these two canals could be joined in some way, the first continuous route, other than the turnpike roads, would be made through the State, and the Eastern and Western States would be put in direct communication. Surveys were started with a view to prolonging the canals over the whole distance, but that idea was abandoned as impracticable. In the year 1831 a law was passed authorizing the Canal Commissioners of Pennsylvania to begin the construction of a "Portage Railroad" from Johnstown to Hollidaysburg, a distance of about thirty-six miles, in which twelve hundred feet of ascent would have to be covered on the western and fourteen hundred on the eastern and steeper slope. Mr. Sylvester Welch was named engineer in charge of the work, Mr. W. Milnor Roberts his principal assistant for the division of the eastern slope, and Mr. Solomon Roberts, to whom we are to-day indebted for our information about the road,* his principal assistant for the western division. The general design, says Mr. Roberts, for the Portage Road was this: "The principal part of the elevation was to be overcome by inclined planes, which were to be straight in plan and profile, to be on an average somewhat less than half a mile long, and to have an angle of elevation of about five degrees, or about the same as moderately steep hills on turnpike roads, so that the average height overcome by each plane might be about two hundred feet. These planes were to be worked by stationary steam-engines and endless ropes. As ultimately constructed, there were ten inclined planes, five on each side of the mountain, and their whole length was four miles and four-tenths, with an aggregate elevation of two thousand and seven feet. * * * The planes were all straight, and the descent on each plane was regular from the top to a point about two hundred feet from the bottom, the last two hundred feet having a gradually diminishing inclination. * * * The

---

* "Reminiscences of the First Railroad over the Alleghany Mountains." Read before the Historical Society of Pennsylvania in 1878, and published in the "Pennsylvania Magazine for History and Biography."

railroad between the planes was located with very moderate grades. * * * It was determined to grade the road at once for a double track, and to build all the bridges and culverts of stone. There was no wooden bridge on the line. In the case of one small bridge of two spans which had to be built at an oblique angle, I proposed an iron superstructure, but the plan was not approved. * * * Great care was taken with the drainage of the road-bed, and a large number of drains and culverts were built, there being one hundred and fifty-nine passages for water under the road."

The road as first used had only one track, with "turn-outs," on the levels, but a double track on the inclined planes. The rails were imported from Great Britain and hauled on trucks from Huntingdon on the Juniata River. "The rails were supported by cast-iron chairs. * * * In most cases these chairs rested upon and were bolted to blocks of sandstone." Many of these blocks, as I have said, are still to be seen embedded in the roadway, from which the rails, of course, have disappeared. "On the inclined planes, which were to be worked by means of ropes, flat bar-rails were laid upon string-pieces of timber. * * * At the head of each plane were two engines of about thirty-five horse-power each. * * * One engine only was used at a time; but two were provided, for greater security. * * * For the prevention of accidents, safety-cars were used upon the inclined planes, which prevented any serious accident, by acting as a drag, or break-shoe, so as to stop the cars and prevent them from running down the plane. * * *

"On the 26th of November, 1833, about two years and a half from the beginning of the work, the first car passed over the road. * * * On the 18th of March, 1834, when canal navigation opened, the Portage Road was opened for use as a public highway, the State furnishing the motive power *on the inclined planes only*, and it continued in use until the canals were closed for the winter. The railroad was again opened on the 20th of March, 1835, shortly after which the second track was completed. * * * The cost of the road at the close of the year 1835 was one million six hundred and thirty-four thousand three hundred and fifty-seven dollars and sixty-nine cents at the contract prices. This did not include office-expenses, engineering, or some extra allowances made to contractors, etc. * * * Nor did it include the cost of locomotives and cars."

The way in which we are told the road was first managed is in curious contrast to the modes of railroad government approved to-day. As has been said, the State furnished the motive power on the planes only. No steam was used on the level tracks, and they were considered public highways, to be traversed by every man as he saw fit. "Every man for himself," says Mr. Roberts, "was considered to be the popular way to run a railroad. * * * Individuals and firms had their own drivers, with their own horses and cars. The cars were small, and had four wheels, and each car would carry about seven thousand pounds of freight. Usually four cars made a train, and that number could be taken up and as many let down an inclined plane at one time, and from six to ten such trips could be made in an hour. * * * The experiment of thus working the road as a public highway was very unsatisfactory. * * * The drivers were a rough set of fellows, and sometimes very stubborn and unmanageable. It was not practicable to make them work by a time-table, and the officers of the railroad had no power to discharge them."

The "popular" mode of procedure was especially unfortunate in its results while there was but one track on the levels between the "turn-outs." So long as this was the case, "a large post, called a centre-post, was set up half-way between two turn-outs, and the rule was made that when two drivers met on the single track with their cars the one that had gone beyond the centre-post had the right to go on, and the other that had not reached it must go back to the turn-out which he had left. The road was in many places very crooked, and a man could not see far ahead. The way the rule worked was this: when a man left a turn-out he would drive very slowly, fearing he might have to turn back, and as he approached the centre-post he would drive faster and faster, to try to get beyond it and drive back any car that he might meet. In this way cars have been driven together and a man killed by being crushed between them."

It did not take very long for the people to be convinced that this was not the best way of managing things. The Canal Commissioners' report for 1837 speaks of "the excitement which has been up against the inclined planes of the commonwealth," and says it arose "from the bad management they had received. The delays and accidents that attended them resulted from inexcusable or willful negligence, and were not chargeable to failure in the planes to accomplish what had been expected of them." Very soon the use of horses was entirely done away with.* The first locomotive used on a level was "a light engine with one pair of driving-wheels, which were made of wood with iron hubs and tires. The fuel used was wood, and the engine ran readily around short curves, and, although its power was not great, the machine worked well and gave satisfaction." The engines, of course, did not pass over the planes. After steam was introduced along the whole line of the route, the time consumed to transfer passengers over its thirty-six miles was about four hours.

An account of the tribulations of the engineer corps during the progress of the work gives us an idea of the savage nature of the district even fifty years ago. Traveling had to be done on foot all along the line of work, and it may be conceived that it was not trav-

---

* There is a discrepancy in our authorities as to just when this occurred. Mr. Roberts says, in 1835 already; but in the Commissioners' report for 1837 their use is strongly recommended, and the engineer promises to introduce them as soon as possible.

eling of a very comfortable kind. The surface of the country was very rough, and progress much impeded by fallen timber. The work was begun by clearing a track one hundred and twenty feet wide through a dense forest of heavy spruce and hemlock. The climate was very severe, and in summer the insects were a terrible scourge and rattlesnakes were so plenty that the chief amusement of the workmen consisted in catching them alive.

In spite of all the difficulties coincident with the building of a road through a pathless wilderness, urged on by the haste of a pressing public need, and shackled to a certain extent by State interference and the bickerings of political parties, Mr. Roberts says, reviewing the work after a lapse of fifty years, and in all the light that more recent achievements have thrown upon it, "It appears to me that the locating was about as well done as could be expected under the circumstances as they then existed. Railroad construction was a new business, and much had to be learned from actual trial; but it was known at the time that the location was too much hurried, which arose from the great impatience of the public. A good deal of curvature might have been avoided by a careful revision of the line, but the reduction of the height of the summit by a tunnel, as has since been done, the Legislature refused to permit. * * * At that time the importance of straightness in a railroad was not adequately appreciated." The summit of the Portage Road, at the present village of Summitvile, was two thousand three hundred and twenty-two feet above mean tide, or one hundred and sixty-one feet higher than the level of the present tunnel at Gallitzin.

"We were striving," says the engineer, "to build a great public work to endure for generations, and, as it turned out, it was superseded by something better in about twenty years. * * * I may here mention the fact that in 1851 the State began the construction of a road to avoid the inclined planes, with a maximum grade of seventy-five feet per mile, and a summit tunnel about two thousand feet long.* Parts of the old line were used, and the road was lengthened about six miles. A single track was laid down, and was in use in 1856, but in the following year the whole work, as a part of the main line, was sold to the Pennsylvania Railroad Company."

Work intended to last for generations does indeed seem to have ill fulfilled its object, admirably as it played its part at the time and indispensable as it then was, when one is obliged to record that not only the original Portage Road but also this later work, known as the "New Portage," has ranged itself among the almost-forgotten relics of the past. Even the long summit tunnel is abandoned, I am told, though the one in use to-day runs very near it. Another tunnel belonging to the first road and cutting through a spur of the mountain three miles east of Johnstown, nine hundred and one feet in length and about twenty feet in width and height, has also been long deserted. It surely deserves a better fate than the premature oblivion which has overtaken it, from the fact that it was *the first railroad-tunnel* in the United States. A citizen of Johnstown amused me not long ago by relating the dangerous feat he accomplished by driving through it in a buggy, a thing which no one, to his knowledge, had attempted for many years. The darkness, of course, was utter, and the risk arose from the possible previous falling of rocks to block the way or upset his carriage, and from the washing of holes in the roadway. The only structure connected with either portage now put to service is, I believe, the great viaduct which was

* Long before this—so early as the year 1837, indeed—we find that the doing away with the planes had already been discussed. The Canal Commissioners for that year combat the project, while acknowledging the fact that it would have been wiser in the beginning to have so constructed the road. It is amusing, in comparison with the way time is considered on the railroads of to-day, to note their explanation that at the best *only* an hour and a half could be gained by the change,—in a distance of thirty-six miles!

the pride of the older route, and which crosses the bend of the Conemaugh eight miles east of Johnstown. It is very substantial and handsome, seventy-five feet in height, with a single semicircular arch of eighty feet span, and built of light-colored, dressed sandstone. The lover of the picturesque may be excused for preferring its solid beauty to the effect of an iron structure of the kind that would now be erected by the railroad in such a place.

If we drive once more from the Summit down toward Hollidaysburg, we shall see portions of the old road which are now inaccessible to wheels, but which sometimes form most exquisite bridle-paths. The roadway passes now under, now over, the turnpike by means of the viaduct-arches of which I have spoken, and its grass-grown track appears and disappears in the most perplexing manner. Numerous trips up and down the mountain will, indeed, scarcely leave us with more definite ideas than we had in the beginning as to just what course this part of the road pursued when it was in working order.

A MISSIONARY PRINCE.

In no State has a greater number or variety of nationalities gone to make up a now Americanized population than in Pennsylvania. And in no county is this better exemplified than in Cambria. It contains to-day, of course, many men of all nations and from all sections of our own, drawn thither by its vast mining and manufacturing industries. But, in addition to this, we shall find, if we go back to the history of its first settlement, that it was peopled, not from one source, and not by chance accretions from many sources, but mainly by three distinct waves of immigration. First we hear of Pennsylvania Germans from the eastern part of the State, who settled the westerly portion of the county about Johnstown. Then came large numbers of American Catholics from Maryland and the adjacent parts of Pennsylvania, many of them descendants of the famous colony of Lord Baltimore. These established themselves at Loretto, as it came afterward to be called, and in its vicinity. They were in part of Irish and in part of German extraction. The third important source of population was a large party of sturdy Welshmen, fresh from their mother-country, who founded Ebensburg, now, as then, the county seat, and named both it and the county itself. Their history is that of common-place prosperity, and it is not of them nor of the German Protestant colony that I would speak in detail, but of the Catholic community, around the annals of which clusters all the poetry of a district much wider than Cambria County, —if indeed by such a name I may call the tales of poverty and privation and rough endeavor, of superstition and self-sacrifice and fervid piety, which form the historical and legendary treasure of the Alleghenies.

The early settlers of the Allegheny would, however, be passed over with but scant attention amid the mass of similar pioneers who have smoothed the rough ways and made plain the paths for us from side to side of our broad continent, were not their struggles and successes identified so closely with the name of Gallitzin, in whose story there are elements of romance and striking lights of contrast such as we do not find very often even in the biography of a missionary priest. Others have been as bold, as self-denying, as rudely tried and poorly rewarded, as he, and have accomplished as much or more in the way of practical results. But of none, I think, can it be said that he was so isolated in his work or so exclusively entitled to the credit of the results. And it is certain that few men have given up so much as he for their work's sake. It is the brilliant story of his early youth, and the thought of the splendid career that might have been his had he not freely chosen his lonely and toilsome lot, that cast about the memory of Demetrius, Prince Gallitzin, and arish priest of Loretto, a tinge of romance that is wanting to the tory of even his most adventurous and most devoted compeers.*

The name of Gallitzin is familiar in our ears, not through the xploits of one famous man, but from its constant recurrence in the nnals of Russia, borne by a succession of soldiers and statesmen igh for many generations in the offices and honors of their native and. The father of our prince was born in 1728, and was a diplo-nate in the service, successively, of the Empresses Elizabeth, Anna, nd Catherine II. He was ambassador for fourteen years at Paris, vhere he was the friend of Voltaire, D'Alembert, and Diderot, and fterward at the Hague, where his son was born in 1770. The only ther child was a sister older than Demetrius, or, to use the pretty ussian diminutive by which he was called, "Mitri." The prince's vife was Amalia von Schmettau, daughter of the celebrated Prussian ield-marshal and sister of the general of that name. She was a woman f fine mind and the strongest character.† Although beautiful, young, nd *fêted*, she withdrew after a very few years from all society save uch as furthered her purpose, with the intention of educating herself nd her children. Residing apart from her husband, who was de-ained at his post by the duties of his position, but always in the nost friendly communication with him, she traveled all over Europe vith her children, settling wherever the prospects seemed best for he thorough training she had planned, and which she always super-ntended herself. The greater part of Mitri's school-days were spent t Münster, in Westphalia, where there was a Catholic college. The

---

* A biography of Gallitzin was written a number of years ago by a German riest named Lemcke. The materials contained therein, together with much new natter drawn from the prince's own papers, have been used by Miss Sarah H. Brownson in her "Life of Gallitzin," published in 1873. From this most interest-ng book the greater number of the following facts have been selected.

† Dr. Katercamp's life of this princess, and her own "Tagebuch und Brief-wechsel," may be consulted for an account of a woman remarkable even in that y of striking personalities.

princess chose it not at all for sectarian reasons, for she had never professed to believe in any form of Christianity and had never instructed her children in religion, but solely for its superior advantages as a place of secular training. Through long association with its professors, however, she was at last induced to embrace Catholicism, after, as we are told, having studied and meditated on the subject for three years from the time when she first acknowledged its claim upon her attention. It is needless, perhaps, to say that, with her strong mind and quick emotional nature, she became the most enthusiastic of devotees and the most indefatigable of propagandists. Many years later she was instrumental in bringing into her Church the Count von Stolberg, whose conversion stirred political and philosophical Germany from end to end, and who became himself the instrument of the no less noted conversion of Friedrich von Schlegel.

In the year 1787, when he was seventeen years old, the young prince joined his mother's church. Strangely enough, the fact gave her little pleasure at the time, for such seemed then to her to be the weakness and indecision of his character that she regarded the profession of his faith rather as a proof of thoughtlessness or pliability than as a vital and determinate act. His father was deeply grieved at the occurrence. Mitri had been intended from his birth for a Russian officer, and had been educated with that end in view. His father, a man of fine intellect and upright character, had no belief in religion of any sort, but knew that it was wise—indeed, in a manner, requisite—that a Russian soldier should profess, if any, the Greek faith of his countrymen. He could but trust that time would accomplish what his wife feared it might, and prove Mitri's conversion but a freak or a temporary mood of thought.

Mitri's education finished, there were still two years to spare ere he could enter upon the active exercise of his profession. Many plans for improving them were suggested, none of which could be carried into effect, owing to the disturbed state of Europe, where the French Revolution had just broken out. After much discussion, it was decided that he should go to America, to study the new republic which had so recently drawn the eyes of Europe upon itself. General Von Schmettau suggested that he should give his nephew letters to Washington and put him under the personal supervision of the first President. But this was opposed, for reasons that to-day seem strange enough to be amusing and, I think, worth quoting. Von Fürstenberg, the founder of the college at Münster, writes to the princess: "It is true we have aimed throughout Mitri's whole education to secure him against the blind following of strange views or prejudices; but he is young, weak, and vain. The fame of Washington is dazzling for him: he would very likely accept his opinions, even his manners, out of veneration for him and to please him. We know the impression a famous man makes upon a youth; but who of us has any knowledge of Washington's *religious and moral principles, of his political honesty?*" At last the young prince embarked from Rotterdam, under the charge of a priest, and with letters recommending him to the care of Bishop Carroll, of Baltimore, "the father of the Church in America."

Scarcely had he touched the shores of Maryland, we are told, when he made up his mind to abandon Europe and his brilliant career, his family and friends, and the society of his equals in things social and intellectual, and enter upon the life of a missionary priest, buried in the heart of a vast wilderness and surrounded only by people who were in all cases rough and uncultivated and in some cases quite uncivilized. It seems impossible that such a decision should have been arrived at by a youth of twenty-two without some strong outside influence brought to bear. There seems to have been something of delay and a spirit that was a little less than frank in the way the news of his project was communicated to his friends at Münster, through them to his mother, and through her to

Prince Gallitzin. The princess did not receive the news with pleasure, as her son had hoped she might, for, as before, she doubted his constancy and strength of mind. It was a year ere she was convinced he had done wisely, but then she entered heart and soul into his plans, without, apparently, a selfish thought bestowed upon the fact that he was lost to her for this world. His father's displeasure and grief can be readily imagined. An only son, the hope of his race no less than the pride of his immediate family, to bury himself in the bosom of an alien Church, and the depths of an almost unknown and distant land! Authority at a distance would have had but little effect; yet the way in which the disappointed father resigns himself to the inevitable and expresses his affection for the son who has so blasted his hopes is so sturdy and so noble that most of our sympathy with the participants in the triangular family discussion goes with him.

In three years after his landing on our shores, the young prince had completed his seminary course, taken the lower orders, and been consecrated priest. From the courage and intrepidity with which he grappled ever afterward with the toils and dangers and persecutions of his life, we should conclude that it was a desire for combat and exertion that had led him to embrace his vocation, were we not told that he himself explained his decision as having resulted from the unquiet, convulsed state of Europe as compared with the "tranquil, peaceable, and happy situation of the United States, together with some consideration, naturally suggested by these events, on the vanity of worldly grandeur and preferment." He was the first priest whom the Catholic Church in this country could claim as entirely her own, having been both educated and consecrated on her soil.

The exact extent of the sacrifice that Gallitzin made when he embraced a life of missionary work cannot be understood without a fuller description of the state of the country and of the Church than

I can enter into here. The first Catholic colony had been founded at Baltimore in 1634. All the churches in the country remained under the charge of the vicar-general of London until the Revolution, and the first bishop, Carroll, was appointed in 1789 only. It is hard to picture to ourselves the then distressed and disorganized condition of a Church now so flourishing. The Catholic population was widely dispersed and miserably poor,—made up, moreover, of the most discordant elements. Its clergy were foreigners of all sorts, and unable, very often, to sympathize with—even to speak intelligibly to—the congregations under their charge. At first, Gallitzin was an itinerant missionary,—indeed, few priests at that time were anything more,—wandering through vast tracts of the roughest country in Maryland, Virginia, and Pennsylvania. Many legends are told connected with this period of Gallitzin's life, detailing how he cast out very palpable devils and overcame with supernatural aid of the most visible kind all doubting inquirers with whom he came in contact, and obstinate heretics who had never even gone so far as to doubt. The spiritualistic stories of to-day do not exceed in fantastic detail and apparently well-authenticated endorsement these last century tales of possessing spirits, of warning, threatening voices, and of clear, prophetic visions.

A TOILER IN THE WILDERNESS.

In 1799, after four years of incredible hardship, during which he had become thoroughly acquainted with the character both of the country and its people, he obtained permission to settle in the remotest district of Pennsylvania which the Church had yet invaded, the wildest, rudest, and most uninviting in all save the grandeur of its scenery and the fertility of its soil when once cleared of its tremendous forest-growth. At the place which he afterwards named

Loretto he built a little church of logs, which was dedicated with a solemn midnight mass, chanted in his magnificent voice on Christmas eve. The scene as we picture it is one of wild beauty no less than of impressive solemnity. His hearers had gathered from places within a radius of scores of miles. Some were members of his flock; others, ruder and more ignorant still, had been drawn by rumors of an unaccustomed spectacle. They were as unlike the young soldier and courtier turned priest as was the rough little structure lined with evergreens stuck full of shining candles to the palaces where he had been born and bred. The snow, we are told, was waist-deep outside the church.

I have no space to follow in detail the long record of the life and labors of Gallitzin, or "Father Smith," as for many years he was called, allowing no mention of his real name and rank to be made. At Loretto he dwelt till his death in 1840, leaving his immediate charge only to make toilsome and dangerous journeys still farther into the heart of the wilderness, where there was not even a log church to receive him, but where service was performed, often for the benefit of a single family, in kitchen, barn, or stable. For very short visits he went only at the rarest intervals and on necessary business to Baltimore and Philadelphia. More than once he refused tempting suggestions of preferment, even of the mitre itself. His desire had from the first been to build up a community trained, ordered, and governed in the strictest accordance with the precepts of Christianity and the Church, free from that alloy of worldliness which to all but enthusiasts appears an inevitable ingredient in human communities. He undertook a vast task, for he constituted himself in the fulfillment of it the guide and ruler of his people in their worldly as in their spiritual concerns. He was imperious, doubtless, very often, but only with the worldly scoffer and the unrepentant evil-doer. With all others he was as tender and humble as the lowliest woman. Autocrat as he grew to be over his scattered and incongruous flock, where the Irish and the German elements were never long at peace, can we wonder that he became an object of persecutions, slanders, envyings, and jealousies of every kind? His rule was denounced as tyrannical, even unjust; his motives were questioned, his private character assailed, complaints were carried time and again to the bishop, and a rival settlement, with a rival priest, established itself at his very doors. His patience, firmness, and meekness combined seemed to have been almost superhuman, and they conquered entirely in the end. At the time of his death his enemies were silenced,—many of them, indeed, converted into his warmest adherents. His death was lamented far and wide as a public calamity.

The persecutions which he was forced to endure were not a tenth part so distressing to Father Gallitzin, however, as the pecuniary troubles which came upon him without any fault of his own save that he trusted in the promises of his friends at home. His father, who died in 1803, always maintained that his son had formally renounced all claims on the estate. This the son as firmly denied. The property all went to the princess, who, finding that on account of his apostasy and expatriation she could leave no part of it safely to her son, bequeathed it at her death, in 1806, to her daughter, who promised to share it equally with Demetrius. In order to make sure that it would go to the Princess Mimi, and not to collateral relations, Gallitzin was urged by his mother to come home for a time and attend to the legal transactions himself. This he at first thought of doing, but finally concluded that a separation from his struggling flock would be too great a wrong to them. His allowance came but sparingly and at long intervals. It is impossible to decide to-day whether the blame was wholly due then and later to the disturbed state of Europe and the difficulty of remitting money with safety, or in part at least to the culpable negligence of his sister and her various agents. Suffice it to say that he never received the portion of the estate which his mother had promised him and his sister had sworn to deliver over, and never saw his way clear to go home and claim it for himself. When he first settled at Loretto, and was in constant expectation of large remittances from home, he judged that the best way to insure the speedy settlement and steady prosperity of the parish would be to buy large tracts of land in his own name and sell them again in small portions and at low rates, to be paid for at the convenience of purchasers. Part of the land, moreover, he retained in his own hands as a trust property, which should in future insure a sufficient income for the Church's establishment at Loretto. Owing to his failure, in spite of constant promises, to obtain any but a comparatively small portion of the large fortune that should have been his, financial embarrassment pursued him through the whole course of his life. It is easy to say that he was in constant terror for years lest a very short time would see his total ruin, but it is not so easy to imagine his feelings during those years when he felt that ruin for him would be ruin as well for his beloved church establishment and for hundreds of poor people whom he loved and who had confided in his judgment, who had even come into the wilderness at his solicitation. This last bitter trial was spared him, and when he died his Church was flourishing. His dreams of her educational establishments have realized themselves, whatever may be said of the surrounding community that was to have been so true a model of a Christian people. The Catholics around Loretto to-day, in so far as a stranger can judge, are about like the Catholics—and Protestants—to be found elsewhere.

Loretto is only some five miles distant from Cresson, and is situated on the slope of one of those broad, shallow vales which are so characteristic of the Allegheny. Gallitzin's rude little home, with its adjoining chapel, is still intact, but the church of his day has been replaced by a great brick structure, in front of which stands his monument. Near it is a large building, where the Sisters of Mercy have a boarding-school, and on the opposite slope of the valley, buried in trees, is a college under the direction of the Franciscan Brothers, whither young men come from all parts of the country to be educated. In the midst of the smiling prosperity of the region, and remembering the importance to the whole country of the institutions that Gallitzin founded, we find it hard to believe that only eighty years have passed since he consecrated his little log chapel, and that it was then the only sanctuary of his faith between Lancaster and St. Louis.

THE LAND OF MINE AND FURNACE.

When we have made acquaintance with all that Cambria County has to show in the way of antiquities and natural beauty,—when its lovely drives have become familiar, when the Portage Road and its ruins have been studied, when we have visited Loretto and the name of Gallitzin is well known and well beloved, when we have dined at that shady little inn in Ebensburg which recalls the "Golden Lion" or the " Stork " or "Palm-Branch" of some German village,—there is still much remaining in the vicinity to attract us. If we care for modern industries,—for man as well as nature, and his present work as well as his past history,—if we can amuse and instruct ourselves with the problems and triumphs of practical science, there could be no better field for us than this. From the mining of coal and iron to the final processes by which the latter is transformed into shapes the most complicated, the most delicate, and the most ingeniously serviceable to man, there is no stage of the labor which may not be studied within the distance of an hour's journey from Cresson. The whole country is underlaid with beds of ore and metal. As we drive down to Hollidaysburg amid the relics of the "Portage" and over the steep, wooded roads, we come at short intervals on dark holes in the mountain-side, or long "shoots" to bring the material down from a higher level to the turnpike. Here coal is dug for local consumption, and is transported in winter on sledges to the farmer's very door. Lilly is a large mining village, right on the line of the present railroad. Its streets are filled with begrimed men, their faces and their clothes of a uniform sooty complexion, and each wearing the tiny lantern which the world over is the miner's badge. One is almost disappointed not to hear the hearty "*Glück auf!*" which is the miner's specific greeting in every part of the Fatherland, and which, to those who there first made acquaintance with the grimy fraternity, seems as characteristic of it as the lantern or the coal-dust itself.

But if we would see what a primitive Pennsylvanian mining village and its inhabitants are like, we cannot do better than make the excursion to "Bell's Gap," which is locally celebrated for the beauty of the scenery. Running down the railroad to a point a few miles east of Altoona, we take a little branch road that goes at right angles to the main line, some nine miles up into the mountain-pass. The memory of a magnificent October morning comes to me as I write. A train of empty cars was about to go up for coal, and a sort of little open wagon was attached for our accommodation *in front* of the engine. It might have been a somewhat dangerous mode of traveling had the speed been great, and even where it took us fifty minutes to cover the nine miles it was, at all events, an exciting mode. Around the edge of the mountain we crept, crossing from the side of one peak to the side of its neighbor over fragile, many-storied trestles. To every finger-tip we felt each throb of reserved power in the body of the docile giant so close behind us. But a strength so near at hand seemed to become part of ourselves, and, with the free view of the snake-like rails before us, we felt we were, in some occult, inspiring way, the authors of our own smooth, resistless progress. Mist on the mountain-tops, shadows of cloud, and gleams of sun through the valleys brought out the autumn tints most beautifully. Brighter single trees—more scarlet maples, for instance, and ruddier oaks—I had seen in other places in other years, but I had never seen a place where the rolling hills formed such superb vistas, where the various trees were so exquisitely blended, where the proportion of evergreens was so exactly right, and where the peaks and slopes had been so little disturbed by the charcoal-burner's axe, or by the fire that has scarred so much of the Adirondack country and so many miles along Lake George. The trees were in fullest leaf, and scarce two of the same kind seemed to grow together,--so that the shape of each was defined as far as the eye could see it against the slightly-contrasting colors of its neighbors. And these colors I had never seen so exquisitely delicate, so variously shaded. There was no violence, not a crude tint, but the very perfection of bright browns, and dull reds, and yellows both dull and bright,—yellows as deep and permanent-looking as the green of the pines, or as evanescent and fairy-like as the mist that crept among them.

There is no view from the end of the line. The road runs its head into the mountain-side, where lie the treasures that it seeks. A cluster of gray-painted frame houses forms the nucleus of the village. The forest-paths on every hand are straggling streets of ruder dwellings — simple log huts or board shanties, which make one shiver to think of long winters spent within their paper walls.

The men are at work in the mines, and our attention must needs confine itself to the women of the village and such stray members of the working sex as are either above or below the grade of a miner. There are some rather ruffianly-looking ne'er-do-weels whom one ranks at once in the last-named class, while social superiority is represented by the country doctor and attorney and the capitalist—

judge or general, I have forgotten just what the title happened to be --whose name distinguishes more than one locality in the neighborhood. The artist who would fill his sketch-book with rustic figures from such a scene as this must be content with the individual, and that only of a grotesque kind: he must look neither for beauty nor for picturesqueness. There is nothing to be seen among the women which even hints of a beauty past, present, or possible of imagining. There is no delicate grace suggested, such as we see developed in our own better classes. There is none of the rugged and healthy womanhood we have seen among the peasantry of other lands. And there is scarce a trace of the neat and self-reliant alertness which so often makes a homely, middle-aged New-England woman attractive to all observers. The types are not only unbeautiful, but most uninteresting. There is seldom an appearance of health, never a look of neatness. Almost every woman looks unhappy, and all look tired and worn and ill and dull. Here on the top of the mountain there can be no malaria to give this look we know so well among the farming population of the lowlands of the West. But the pure air is probably no sufficient antidote against the bad food and hard labor and severe cold with insufficient shelter which form the basis of this monotonous existence.

No two towns could be less alike than the two which are chief in Cambria County,—Ebensburg and Johnstown. The former lies quietly at the end of a tiny branch line, sleepy and old and Catholic and agricultural. The latter is divided by the rails of the great highway itself, and is new, rough, and busy with the rush of huge mills and factories and the throb of perpetually-passing trains. It is not dusty like Ebensburg, but grimy; not breezy, but smoky; not spread on top of the mountain, but cramped into a six-sided little valley at the junction of two rivers. Steep hills enclose it almost entirely, their wooded sides visible in every direction over the house-tops. The gap in the mountain where the river finds a westerly exit is filled, as we see it from the town, by the railway viaduct and the Cambria Iron Works' many chimneys with their banks of smoke. The town is but a dependence of the works and of the minor industries which have grown up about them. The few fine residences are owned by men high in the company's service and rich with its earnings, while the streets of countless little dwellings, each with a family likeness to the other, tell of a long roll of workmen busy in its mills or in the coal-mines that feed them, disgorging their black nutriment almost directly into the gaping furnace-mouths. If we climb one of the long, winding, yet very steep hill-roads and reach the level table-land that spreads its fields and forest broadly toward the west, we soon see a different style of farm from the small holding and shabby little tenement of the mountain farmer. The Cambria Company, securing its mineral rights, thought best to buy the property out and out, and, farming it principally for hay crops for its own consumption, shows it to us in broad clover-fields beautiful in their extent and neatness.

The tourist who travels for pleasure only does not often stumble on such hostelries as those which afford us accommodation in Johnstown. Here we may make, perhaps, our first acquaintance with the provincial hotel, kept, not for the tourist or the summer boarder, but for the commercial traveler. The preternaturally early breakfast-hour and the twelve o'clock dinner tell of business habits which we had thought extinct with a previous generation. Whatever else may be missing from the bedrooms, we are sure to find in each a long extension-table of many leaves for the use of the errant salesman. Through some open door we can always see one piled high with samples of the latest fashions as adulterated for the provincial market. In 1835, when the "Portage" was being built, Johnstown was a quiet little village clustering about the canal basin and with elderbushes growing high in the main street.

IRON AND STEEL—A BESSEMER BLAST.

The Cambria Company's iron-works are among the largest and best-appointed in the country, and there are, moreover, vast wire-mills in the town, where small articles of many sorts are manufactured from the heavy wire that comes to them from the iron-works proper. One does not soon tire of watching their curious processes, in many of which the clever machine requires no assistance, save that of a boy to see that it does not get out of order. We may watch, for instance, how the barbed wire for fences is prepared by a machine whose working is so simple as to be understood at first sight by the least initiated. Two long wires enter the machine, on top of which lie two others in small coils. As the main wires pass between these two which are to form the barbs, their ends insert themselves between and twist around the main ones, and are then cut off short by a pair of shears which come out to snip at the right moment and then retire with a vicious precision quite comical to see. The long wires then twist themselves together and reel themselves into large coils ready for sale. And all this is done in plain sight, in the twinkling of an eye, by the unaided machine, which takes up no more space, by the way, than an ordinary centre-table.

In contrast to the noise and glare and rush of places where metal in any shape is treated hot are the rooms in the wire-mills where heavy wire is drawn in a cold state into grades of greater tenuity. The machines look not only simple but ineffective in their quiet working, and the absence of fire is the absence of all excitement and picturesqueness. But it is all the more wonderful, perhaps, to see the great wire rods gradually becoming less and less in diameter till they are finished into little shining coils of stuff as fine as a hair and as smooth as a silken thread.

Daylight must be used, of course, to inspect all such minor processes as these. And daylight alone reveals the vast scale on which the main work is prosecuted and permits us to study the *modus* of its action and realize its marvelous results. But at night, when the factories are at rest, the iron-mills roar on, and it is then that their weird impressiveness is best revealed. Night after night, so long as we are within its reach, the infernal attraction lays hold of us and draws us within its fiery circle. Night after night we are bewildered and excited by the rush and noise and force and glare of the gigantic conflict between man and the brute material which he conquers and moulds to his will at last by the well-directed power of his fearful allies, flame and steam.

The great yard at night is a treacherous field of darkness, a labyrinth of tracks, where tiny engines puff and sneeze and jerk about their loads of black or still incandescent metal, rushing hither and thither at tangents impossible to calculate in the enshrouding gloom, and helping us by no civility of head-lights or cautionary signals. For this is their home, their private domain, and when the public intrudes upon it the public is alone responsible for keeping itself out of harm's way. We grope about in a half panic toward one or another of the vast buildings which flank the yard on all its sides, some silent and dark, some disgorging light and noise in all profusion. On the one hand tower the vast stacks of the blast-furnaces, which roar day and night through uninterrupted months for their endless meal of ore and fuel. Far off in another direction the long, low rolling-mills show through their open doors a red-hot interior, with black, hurrying figures and winding streaks of fiery metal. But dominating the whole, brighter and fiercer and noisier than all, are the Bessemer steel-works, and here we stop first to see the very apotheosis of our century,—an apotheosis of iron, water, fire, and their forces in resistless combination. Mr. Ruskin has done what he could to disgust us with steam, its processes and its results. We wait for a subtler and more daring critic to point out its superb picturesqueness, its imaginative and artistic side. We cannot fail, however, to realize them for the moment if we stand awhile on this little platform high up on one side of the huge raftered building where the Bessemer blast is in progress. From this platform a boy controls with half a dozen levers the hydraulic forces which lift and lower and swing the machinery of giant cranes and buckets and ingots and converters with which the tiny, hurrying human figures do their task. The ruddy glare reveals all the infernal beauty of the scene, but covers up and glorifies the dirt and grime we know must be there. We follow this "Bessemer process,"—the most grandly picturesque, perhaps, of all the processes by which metal is treated,—not for scientific but for æsthetic satisfaction. We see one end of the building taken up by a vast accretion of chimneys and troughs and ladders and platforms. In front, just under the great, gaping chimney-mouths high up in the air, hang two huge cylindrical receptacles,—the "converters,"—into which the hot iron is poured to be deprived entirely of its carbon and then doctored by the addition of a certain given quantity thereof,—which addition of just the right amount transforms it into steel. There are other processes for securing the proper quantum of carbon, and no more, to the metal under treatment. But, whatever may be the relative scientific and practical success of this which has made the name of Bessemer famous, there is, picturesquely speaking, no process to be even remotely compared with it. The converters, in alternation, are tipped down to be filled with a stream of fluid iron, and, as they are tilted up into place beneath the chimney-mouth, the whole building is filled with a shining rain of sparks, each like a distinct and much-magnified snow-crystal. The blast of air which is to bear away the carbon is forced through the contents of the converter, to bellow from its top up the chimney and out into the sky above with a deafening roar and a blinding glare. For some fifteen minutes the blast continues, the color and intensity of the immense flame varying as the metal loses its carbon. From these variations of tint and density the "blower" who superintends it judges how the blast progresses, and knows when to give the signal for tipping and emptying the converter just as the carbon is all exhausted and before the metal is burned. As the converter swings down,—controlled, as I have said, by the little lever at our elbow,—all the glare that has gone before seems as darkness compared with that from the incandescent metal pouring into the huge ingot-mould awaiting it. The colors of the liquid, almost etherealized metal in the different stages of the process are as various as they are beautiful,—now red of many grades, now orange, now pale yellow, and sometimes, when seen in little streams, a lavender too intense for steady gazing.

The rail-mill, where the short, thick bars of metal are rolled out in a few moments into the requisite length and shape, is picturesque enough, but in the wire-mill we shall see a sight as remarkable for grace and fascination as the Bessemer blast is remarkable for power and impressiveness. A long line of "rolls," through which the metal is successively passed, stretches across an iron-floored space, and in front of them stand a row of lads ready with their tongs to catch and control the end of the fiery-wire in its swift passage. The thick bar passes between the revolving cylinders which constitute the first pair of rolls, and comes out attenuated to a certain extent. The end is caught in the tongs and inserted between the next pair, passing through, of course, in a reverse direction to that in which it has traversed the first. This process is repeated a number of times, the wire growing thin and long with supernatural rapidity. The longer it grows, the more "slack," so to speak, there is to be controlled as it issues from one pair of rolls to be inserted in the next. It is this which makes the process so strikingly picturesque to the observer and so dangerous to the operator. Yards upon yards of the graceful, serpentine stuff, which looks so pliable but is so stiff and jerky and intractable, accumulate between the pairs of rolls, and with the motion of his tongs the workman must control it so that it neither entangles itself nor injures him. When the end of the process approaches and the length of the wire is very great, the services of another workman are required to seize the slack with his tongs and run backward with it across the iron floor, while his comrade manages the end. The long coils rise and waver high in the air in their rapid flight with a grace that is indescribable, and cover the ground with huge, fiery, snake-like curves in swiftest motion. All the rolls are running at once, of course, a fresh bar being started as soon as the preceding one has left the first pair of rolls; and the wild motions of the metal itself and of the many lads who struggle with it in its apparently frantic efforts to free itself from their control make an exciting spectacle from which it is almost impossible to tear ourselves away. We watch for an ending, a lull which will relax our interest; but the always-beginning, never-ending process continues without a break. There is no small sense of personal danger to add its spice to our enjoyment. It seems momentarily impossible that the burning streak should not get the mastery and cease to coil itself so safely near our feet. Accidents to the rollers seem always imminent, and are, indeed, more frequent here than in any other part of the works. A false step in the backward run over the slippery iron floor is surely disastrous. An end of wire missed by the tongs means, very likely, a hole through arm or body. And not very long ago, we are told, a workman got himself *inside* instead of outside the immense coil that formed and wavered over his head as he inserted the end of the wire between the rolls. In a moment he was cut in twain as the swift revolution drew the metal line taut against the machine. Dangerous as the labor is, it seems strange that lads and quite young boys should usually undertake it. We are told, however, that their greater quickness and agility stand them in better stead than would the presumably cooler heads of their elders. As the wire issues finished from the last "pass," the end is again caught and presented to a wheel which reels it up into the coils we know in our shops, and it is then thrown aside to cool. Long in the telling, this process is swift enough in reality. It takes some forty-five seconds only for the bar to enter the first pair of rolls, traverse them all, be coiled up as five hundred feet of wire, and tossed aside to make room for the next-comer, which is already awaiting the services of the wheel.

The night is far advanced when we cross the yard once more. It is partly lit at times by the glare from the Bessemer chimneys, and anon covered with utter darkness as the converter is tilted down for a while. Leaving its dangers at last behind us, we pass along the bank of the river under the great railroad viaduct which spans it. A solitary locomotive, symmetrical, polished, docile, glides slowly over our heads. Surely it is alive in this magic midnight,—a living, magnificent child of steam and iron and man's intelligence. Gigantic level rays from the Bessemer building far behind us fall upon it and on the rocky river-bed and the huge bridge-arches, and across and beyond them up to the wooded hill-side, where the hoarse voices of the miners and the occasional flashing of their lights show that coal is mined as well as burned by night. Is there no poetry in our nineteenth century and its work? Is there no majesty, no impressiveness, no food for the imagination, in its iron, and steam, and flame, and speed, and power?

REPRINTED FROM LIPPINCOTT'S MAGAZINE.

www.ingramcontent.com/pod-product-compliance
Lightning Source LLC
Chambersburg PA
CBHW032140080426
42733CB00008B/1146
9783744735667